Who is My Neighbor?

by Barbara L. Luciano

PEARSON

Scott
Foresman

Editorial Offices: Glenview, Illinois • Parsippany, New Jersey • New York, New York
Sales Offices: Needham, Massachusetts • Duluth, Georgia • Glenview, Illinois
Coppell, Texas • Sacramento, California • Mesa, Arizona

You live in a community.

A community has homes.

A community can be large.

A community can be small.

A community has signs.

Where do you live?

Glossary

community where people live

large big

sign something that gives people information

small little